Sticks and Stones
CONQUERING HATERS
...with poetry

By
Z.E. Frey

© 2012

STICKS AND STONES
CONQUERING HATERS WITH POETRY

Sticks and Stones, Conquering Haters with Poetry

ISBN-13 978-1475056518

ISBN-10 1475056516

Copyright © 2012

An

I.W.A.

project.

Copyright © 2012

iwa.yolasite.com

Library of Congress in Publication Data

Jerome, Zorina Exie

How To Conquer Haters

Copyright © September 1997

Written by Zorina Exie J. Frey

Edited by Zorina Exie J. Frey

BY Z.E. FREY

All rights reserved.

This book is based on some true events, however, has been fictionalized and all persons appearing in this work are fictitious. Any resemblance to real people, living or dead, is entirely coincidental.

No part of this book may be reproduced or transmitted in any form or by any means, electronic or mechanical, including photocopying, recording, or by any information storage and retrieval system without written consent of the author except where permitted by law.

STICKS AND STONES
CONQUERING HATERS WITH POETRY

CONTENTS

Prologue	6
Whatever	7
A Summary of Some of Me	10
The Root of an Issue	12
Glory Seekers	15
Copy Cats	18
What Do You Want From Me	20
Busybodies	22
On the Other Hand	25
Inspiration	30
I Won't Apologize!	32
Coming Out	34
Ethnocentric	37
Momma Don't Love No More	39
A Letter	41
No Love Lost	43
Karma	45
Not Much Time	47
The Messenger	49
Itches	51
The Remedy	53

BY Z.E. FREY

On saying much with few words…

"The Ten Commandments contained 297 words…The Bill of Rights is stated in 438 words…Lincoln's Gettysburg Address contained 266 words…A recent federal directive to regulate the price of cabbage… contains 26,911 words."

~Unknown

STICKS AND STONES
CONQUERING HATERS WITH POETRY

Prologue

    These prose poems represent a state of mind. The fact that most if not all of these prose poems are abstract is all a part of generalizing the particular subject at hand. You will find that the only issues being exposed are the situations that undoubtedly resonate with individuals across the country and perhaps, the world. The only reputations exposed are convicted hearts as well as the assumptions of which individual fits what scenario. The only finger-pointing will be the reader's conscience however and to whomever it may apply. This, of course, is entirely up to the reader's discretion.

BY Z.E. FREY

WHATEVER

It's kind of funny how jealousy tries to stick to me like honey.

Nice, sweet, in my face with no trace of emotions.

Jealousy.

Yep, that was my enemy.

Trying to take its abode in me.

Trying to insult me.

Trying to make me believe I'm not what God wants me to be all because I don't click

in corporate America like it thinks I should be.

Please.

I chose a long time ago to journey down the narrow road.

Only a few can make out the path.

Some reject it.

Trying to do the math.

Trying to do it on your own? You better go to the throne!

That means kneeling and forsaking the soapbox.

STICKS AND STONES
CONQUERING HATERS WITH POETRY

Wasn't talking about much but other people's business anyway.

Have it your way, I'll gladly take the highway!

No longer interested.

Got a purpose. Proud of it.

No longer subject to illogical mess. Not locked into the stress. God bless

you, but I've got to be me.

This is a kiss off for those who secretly hate on me.

Indignant because I sometimes speak ebonically. Still

financially better off than you might ever dream to be.

God meets my needs.

Don't go by what you see, but

you still do anyway, and

THAT'S OK!

Whatever it takes to make you feel higher than me is just my stepping stone, see.

That, plus a buck-seventy of me must be heavy to hold up!

I'm putting this issue to rest.

BY Z.E. FREY

You hate me, but I will show love anyway.

Jealousy is as bitter as the grave.

It's a rotting away.

It's not my fault you're that way!

I'm not going to follow you to your grave.

Be mad by yourself.

God's word is my health and my wealth.

God

Bless.

STICKS AND STONES
CONQUERING HATERS WITH POETRY

A SUMMARY OF SOME OF ME

Rage. Anger. Peace. Serenity.
All apart of being human. Someone once said that even the greatest have to suffer sometime.
There is glory in suffering, which would explain why glory-seekers always play the victim.
The fact of the matter is those who suffer hardly ever show it and that is how we shine!
I don't need a trumpet for you to know I'm coming.
I simply arrive.
I've never needed anyone to speak highly of me.
Why should I when I'm already the topic of your conversation?
I've never needed my parents to be somebody in order to be somebody.
Adversaries will try me in this wild mid-west to test...only themselves.
They've assumed.
To be greater than He who lives in me because they think I'm nobody.
Who is she? Where did she come from? Who's her family? What's her 411?

BY Z.E. FREY

Truth is, I've been here all along. I've gone through like any given person in this room.
I've fallen several times, but I've made it through.
But I'm not through.
I move on after I've moved on!
Yet, it's difficult to do when past relationships tag at you, like "How do you do?" and "We have some catching up to do."
And cultural taboos taunt you like, "You're really not black because you lack to show your naps!"
No. Not really
because if you really knew, there would be nothing to know. We'd simply acknowledge each other and move on.
A cluster of folks might lead you to believe you need to be acknowledged in order to succeed. I busted my hump just to be.
Yet, no one really wants to know from which path I've succeeded,
because it wasn't pretty and you wouldn't be proud of me.
I might even burst your bubble of a pleasant reality.
Yet, they find my outcome fascinating!
Glory to The King.
To be rejected because The Truth is unaccepted.

STICKS AND STONES
CONQUERING HATERS WITH POETRY

THE ROOT OF AN ISSUE

We always want what we can't have.

Has it ever occurred to us that the thing

we can't have

is bad for us

for the time being?

We get confused.

believing

seeing is believing. Even

the very elect of us can be fooled.

So, who's to say

which way is the right way?

What makes us go around the same situations daily?

Are we avoiding the thing that makes us strong?

Are we being distracted by another

being distracted? And

so on, and so on?

BY Z.E. FREY

Our lives

continue to go on.

Heart seems to beat strong.

The days seem to go long.

We wonder what's wrong.

We continue to live on. We

roam clueless

unable to understand. We

close our eyes and wake up to make up for the

wrongs we've done. We

need to realize there is

nothing new under the sun. We

run from

our own issues

only to create new ones. We

believe the new one will eliminate the old one.

The old one just gets rooted deeper and deeper.

Compressed and oppressed by the new.

STICKS AND STONES
CONQUERING HATERS WITH POETRY

Mind is bonded

with issues.

BY Z.E. FREY

GLORY-SEEKERS

There is glory in suffering, which is why glory-seekers always play the victim. The irony is, they find the glory, but it's not in them. They find it in those who walk like Him. But they want to ignore it because it doesn't benefit them. So, they cry, yell and scream until someone notices them.

I call it a tantrum.

So easy to play the victim, to run and cry about your hurt feelings with no resolution. For someone to lick your wounds is your resolution.

Your nose is stuck in the air, hollering and hooting. Who are you pursuing and why? Your answer will be put to the test. In the end, was it worth it?

There is glory in suffering, which is why glory-seekers always play the victim.

You whine and moan because life is hard, but the ones who stand silent have been through it all.

STICKS AND STONES
CONQUERING HATERS WITH POETRY

A good dose of humility won't keep you talking for long. However,

I've seen folk's faces get blazed...and still find dumb things to say!

They've had their day, but I guess they need another.

But when it comes right to it, never been sorry, never sincerely apologized. Only performed and recited, line by line. Oh yes, there's certainly a thin line!

If you really love me, then you'd just love me, because love is in a look, a smile, not a stare, performance or sneer. I'm old enough to know this here:

There is glory in suffering, which is why glory-seekers always play the victim.

I've seen more strength in my dying mother's eyes than a bishop, apostle, and elder put together.

BY Z.E. FREY

My tolerance with weak people whining has dropped to zero degrees.

Always been called "cold." Now I know why.

There are glory-seekers and those who suffer.

Glory-seekers will forever seek out glory, while those who suffer strong,
will forever shine.

STICKS AND STONES
CONQUERING HATERS WITH POETRY

COPYCATS

Have you ever wondered why the pessimistic always seem to seek you out?

They love you, hate you, and betray you?

Fooling themselves, convincing you that they're your friend just to gain enough information from you and to use it for their own gain. Never mind they betrayed your confidentiality.

The reality is they needed some material to make themselves appear interesting. Since they don't have an identity, they envy yours. It's like they've stolen your personality!

They repeat what you say with no credibility. It's like they're your evil twin clone and you alone, know their game! They charm and fool everyone with YOUR personality! They become you, in the worst way! It's like they're you, but on a really bad day!

Yet, they lack authenticity. They do what they do but without reason.

Their source is you and your source is you-know-who.

The difference is that their well will run dry, but your source will never run dry because it is God who gave you the eyes to recognize your adversary who is contrary to who you are.

You might inspire a Copycat, but you are a rising star.

BY Z.E. FREY

Now, one might argue if you are their source and your source is God, then why should their well run dry?

Because we are fallible. I'm liable to disturb your reality. I might get myself into a situation you might not agree with.

That Copycat might act as your prototype.

Difference?

You don't believe the hype. You paid your price and this carbon copy wants your original receipt!

I simply encourage them to acknowledge defeat! In this meet, the race is not to the swift.

So it's highly recommended that you mind your own.

Then seek.

And you will find your own.

Gift.

Copycats.

STICKS AND STONES
CONQUERING HATERS WITH POETRY

WHAT DO YOU WANT FROM ME?

What do you want from me?
Haven't heard from you in a while, now you're interested in my business?

My life is no picnic, but if you insist then get ready to hear this.

Deal with it. Tarry to carry the heavy. Stay low to avoid blows that friends who are really foes will throw.

Close the door on Copycats ready to step on your toe.

Note the sarcasm.

Watch your back! Some Jack-ass is ready to attack! Act

like you know and don't despise instruction to function.

It's fuel.

Your function is to move at any given time.

Please be kind to rewind your mind at the set time or else,

the lesson learned will be forfeited.

Acquitted. Likely to forget it. And the test,

you'll have to retake it!

What do you want from me? Haven't heard from you in a while. Now, you're interested in my business?

BY Z.E. FREY

Take these words and put them in your mouth.

Want information? I'll give it to you.

spoon-feed you like a baby crying for food.

Now, go. Run and tell that!

Go. Do what you need to do, Judas.

I'll remain cool as this thing unfolds. Don't go hanging yourself.

You know how the story goes.

As for me, I die to my feelings daily. Resurrection is just in me.

Whoever thinks this is blasphemy knows what they can do for me.

Better yet, be like Joseph's siblings and serve me!

I still come lowly which is why I can speak boldly.

I can talk to you for an hour, and you still won't know me!

So, I ask again,

What do you want from me?

STICKS AND STONES
CONQUERING HATERS WITH POETRY

BUSYBODIES

As an African American, I've been taught to reach for the sky to achieve The American Dream.

Yet for some, even myself, that sky was topped with a glass ceiling. I had no parents to go before me to encourage me, only to warn me of the perils of their narrow teachings. Only what they've been taught.
What was passed down from ancestors
who were never taught
an education.
Yet what can I say when people asked me how I feel about our president?

I feel good. Hopeful. Encouraged. Surprised at how far America has come along.

Disappointed at how I allowed a small cluster of ignorance to discourage me into believing that even with an education, I still didn't make much sense. But this is what happens when you're a minority—not talking of gender or nationality. I'm talking about what you set yourself apart from, see.

Busybodies. They will be 90% your enemy.

You'll discover they won't be much of a friend. A seasonal comrade at best. Watch out! Your friendship will be put to the test and you'll find they've failed because they can't keep their mouth shut and compromised your confidentiality. Not that there's much to hide. It's the principle of trust, you see.

Busybodies are your enemy.

I don't care how nice they appear to be. "Beware of Greeks bearing gifts!"

I don't care what they do, listen to what they say and how they look at you, when you're not looking. They appear to be a little too nice.

Beware of glory-seekers who want to play the victim.

STICKS AND STONES
CONQUERING HATERS WITH POETRY

As you suffer misunderstanding, be careful not to become like them.

You see, my enemy has never been race.

It's principalities. Spiritual wickedness in high places.

Masquerading their faces.

They will turn on you quick just to get a piece of you.

So now that I know I can simply because someone said,

"Yes we can,"

and did!

I realize race was merely a tool of principalities used by Busybodies bearing gifts.

BY Z.E. FREY

ON THE OTHER HAND

It's our time to shine.
Not with vengeance, but with class and common sense.
This is a slap in the face for the secretly racist.
Yes we can, Uncle Sam!
I will eat collard greens, eggs, and ham in a White House!
I will not dine in the out house!
Today I stand, firm and stout.
Black and proud.
I will eat collard greens, eggs, and ham in a White House!

I'm catching animosity from people who don't like me!
Whose failure is mirrored by my success.
Would rather lessen my achievements by suggesting that I might travel South
where I'd be better received because this particular elite would not help me.
He'd rather hand me literature on black companies even though I was commended on my bachelor's commencement.

STICKS AND STONES
CONQUERING HATERS WITH POETRY

On the other hand,
I don't expect special treatment.
I expect help because you're supposed to be my brother. I see no color.
I expected help because I helped myself.
I need your help!
But, since you won't help me, I look to my heavenly father who saved me.
The one who set the black man last so he can be first.
But, I hope some of these black men get it and quit disrespecting women and playing the victim.

On the other hand,
If we want to be equal, then we may be marching ourselves right into the melting pot.
Meaning if we want the majority to melt away their superiority, we must do the same.
We pump our fist talking about treat me equal! *Not realizing we must do the same.*
Dr. Martin Luther King said, "We must FOREVER conduct our struggle on a high plane
of dignity and discipline."
This does not mean we mirror the oppressor.

BY Z.E. FREY

The saying goes; two wrongs don't make a right.

Blacks telling jokes about whites? Oh that's OK?
He can call you the "N" word but she can't?
Is about the same as her calling me the "B" word but you can't.
I, myself, am guilty of that.

So how can I demand equality when I'm not rendering the same toward my sister, brother, or
Or even toward my own country?
Yet, how can I love my brother when he is mass producing Baby's Mothers,
treating me like gutter?
When I call myself a bitch, who wins?
Me or them?

Them Democrats are taking all the blame for a deficit created during a Republicans reign.
Suddenly, they have solutions!
Where were these solutions when they were in office some years ago?

Can a man be a bitch and is it the same as a whore?

STICKS AND STONES
CONQUERING HATERS WITH POETRY

Do we even know what we are fighting for?
Does anybody know what they stand for?

Both sides are so necessary because people are so contrary.
Hot Monday and Cold Sunday.
You see it one way, I'll see it my way.
You believe this, I'll believe that.

Each belief has its conflicts.
Yet, we stand tall in it all and call the other on their bullshit and
then get caught up in it.
Then repent.
Only to find another belief and do it again;
Find the flaw, find another belief.
Find the flaw,
Point fingers and find another belief.

Then repent!

What do we stand for?
The world is so hypocritical.

BY Z.E. FREY

INSPIRATION

I'm your inspiration.

Don't hate me.

Why are you playing?

Don't hate your inspiration.

You're a ten.

Without the one.

I am the one.

You already knew.

That's why you can't come up with anything new.

You keep ciphering and recycling my style and personality, trying to have a style like me.

You sound like a scratched disc that's been played too much.

You play too much!

Get off my cuff!

I think you've had enough.

I've got the up-graded stuff.

STICKS AND STONES
CONQUERING HATERS WITH POETRY

The original.

Something like a sentinel.

Cynicals look pitiful because they thought they were original.

Never said I told you so, but

This flow is telling so,

Watch what you're saying.

I'm your inspiration.

BY Z.E. FREY

I WON'T APOLOGIZE!

I won't apologize for having a lot on my mind. Not speaking to you just to say, "hi," and you going home trying to figure out why.

Not understanding the things I've come face to face with. When I try to explain it, you erase it. Belittle it. Dismiss it. Make it seem as though it is not, so you can come out on top!

You may take things lightly, but I grab a hold to God's word tightly. It might seem a little weird. He who has ears should hear! All I ever talk about is my walk in this Great Commission. The things I've had to deal with. Distractions which had me tripping. Evil spirits trying to get me to miss it. Listening to the wrong things had me feeling unnecessary pains, and tradition rebuking me like I said something vain, and all I'm telling you is what is here. He with ears ought to hear! I'm not criticizing how you've been made. I just know that there has been a way that is made and I'm trying to make my way through all the vain philosophies, false prophecies, homemade

STICKS AND STONES
CONQUERING HATERS WITH POETRY

proverbs, and various explanations of how it worked for you.

Much appreciated, but that was you!

I won't apologize for having a lot on my mind because I don't have time to explain why I do what I do. It doesn't always have to make sense to you!

When it comes right down to it, this walk is a one-on-one thing. I'm not trying to please religious folks who just don't know. I know how my God talks to me, and if you can't feel me, then hear me. Don't take this personally, but since you choose to measure just how far and wide, how deep and tall God's power is in your life,

Then I have no more words for you.

BY Z.E. FREY

COMING OUT

I've been too cautious to say what I really want to say.

I'm coming out of darkness so my light can shine brightly.

Might offend the high-minded and self-righteous.

It's not surprising.

Everything I've aspired to do, they despised it.

How unfortunate some people don't want to be part of it.

Forget it!

I'm coming out of darkness.

The giftings, the lift-me-ups, the shut-the-hell-up, the here-I-come, the Tupac mentality of I don't give a cluck-cluck, I hear chickenheads cluck, I'm not here standing by luck. I'm protected by the The Son. Like the movie 'Carrie,' they've already been laughing at me and they've already been talking about me behind my back through the act of jealousy laced with insecurity.

I'm coming out of darkness to confront some religious foes. Friend, fiend, or foe, I don't care. Just as long as they know I'm coming out of this thing. It's a set time for everything.

So, if you choose to duel, it behooves you to go to prayer school because my feelings die daily. It isn't too much you can say to faze me. You may hate me, but only God can

Sticks and Stones
Conquering Haters with Poetry

break me. Only God can shake me and only God can wake me.

I'm coming out of darkness.

The intimidation, the afraid-of-what-people-may-say. The idolatrous mentality of pleasing man, the please-o-please, the what-do-you-think? The woe-is-me, the it-never-works-for-me.

Shout it out!
Act it out!
Write it out!
Sing it out!
Even dance it out!
Gifts got clout.

No matter what they say the next day.

I'm already planning my next project, OK?

Either with me or against me,

Regardless, I'm doing my thing.

So get ready, get set for the set time.

My time to shine is nigh.

God using me makes me high.

That's why I live for this.

It's ridiculous!

by Z.E. Frey

Not too many people can get with this.

I might sound pompous, but I still come low.

At set times, coming from under.

All the time, coming out.

Coming out of darkness.

Sticks and Stones
Conquering Haters with Poetry

ETHNOCENTRIC

You blame me for those who won't overcome.

Yet, you despise me for achieving.

Black power? No, I'm not racist, but you're just plain two-faced. To complain about a race that is as ignorant as yours. Difference is, you cover up yours and call it "the norm."

Not talking against whites, but whom they call elites, whether in a religious denomination or in a political fleet. In the masses. Whatever, you can kiss my assets!

Maybe instead of complaining about the next dude, why not try to walk a mile in his shoes?

Consider the mindset of a Republican instead of a Democrat. Without a secure country, there will be world war, believe that. Without someone to govern cities, there will be riots, civil war, and contaminated water mixed with feces. You hear me but don't believe me. Please, do not mix me up with a weeping poet without a remedy.

God isn't mad. So, why are you? The bigger they are, the harder they fall. Confidence turned high-mindedness, that's how Lucifer falls. Yet we have the gall to get mad.

If you aren't humble, your walls will crumble. Believe that. I mean that. I've seen that. No man can run from that. Those are just facts!

BY Z.E. FREY

God has my back. Even if my mind draws blank, that's game. Russian Roulette. I spared you, Babe! Place your bets if you want to. Write me off, I dare you. "My enemies will be put to shame, all for the glory of His name. No weapon formed against me will conquer. Not even the quickest tongue can accuse me." Isaiah 56:17. So, what's your purpose in setting to sedate me?

It isn't me—led to tell it like it is. No one's good. No one's perfect. No, not one. You just lost one!

You blame me for those who won't overcome. Yet, you despise me for overachieving. Any good I do makes you grit your teeth. Everything I achieve makes you green with envy.

Maybe it's not me. It's you.

Perhaps whom you really have a problem with, is you.

STICKS AND STONES
CONQUERING HATERS WITH POETRY

MOMMA DON'T LOVE NO MORE

The ghetto is a grassless meadow.
Full of hollering kids,
Runny noses,
Dirty clothes,
Beat-up doors,
Clothes that are torn.
Daddy isn't home anymore.
Momma don't love no more.
She's full of scorn,
Over a child born
Who's not hers but
Her children have a new sibling.
Daddy committed adultery.
Now momma don't love no more.
Her heart is torn.
Her body is worn out from
Childbirth, beatings and hurt feelings.
She needs healing and is looking for it
Through physical healing.
It doesn't work, so she kneels to a
False god that will never answer her.

BY Z.E. FREY

Neglected and rejected,
Momma don't love no more.

STICKS AND STONES
CONQUERING HATERS WITH POETRY

A LETTER

Oh mister preacher man!
Freaky preacher man.
Help me out here, I can't seem to understand.
Why do you go for the younger honeys who act like dummies, who look for a form of godliness but deny the actual power?

Hmm?

You seem to fit the description, so allow me to give the benediction. Your actions are causing friction between the mothers and the daughters. Get the picture?

Oh Misses sneaky-freaky lady!
Chicky-baby.
Chicky-mama.
Causing drama.

Acting high and mighty. Look at you. Hot and bothered, you don't know what to do. Wanting hands layed on. Not for purification but strictly for fornication. Feels like you took a vacation from your current situation that's definitely not changing. The only thing that's changing is the underwear of despair.

Oh mister freaky preacher man!
Help me understand.
Is it easier to preach to a little girl who according to life's experiences
Wets her pants?
No, I'm really trying to understand.

by Z.E. Frey

Does a woman intimidate you with just demands or are you just being a man?

I want to understand, mister freaky preacher man. I still love you, but what you're doing just isn't cool. Sisters are already out here lost. Like a salad, you want to toss. I'm not mad at you because I was there too.

That's why I can see right through you, girl. Over there looking all innocent and cute too. I see it, so what am I supposed to do?

Shake my head, turn my back and talk about you? Or throw my hands up, give up and join the crew? My heart tells me what I really ought to do. It's just so hard when even church folks are doing it too.

So tell me, what do I do? Run away? Or stay and fight another day?

Pray?

Oh yes I do. With patience and perseverance, I still have to look at you.

Sticks and Stones
Conquering Haters with Poetry

NO LOVE LOST

I've had folks piss on my reputation and nemesis suddenly taking an interest in me

because they think I'm no longer a contender. Please.

You better believe as long as I breathe and as long as there's a heartbeat,

I'm still up for what's mine!

I just took time so you can get a piece of mind and maybe an identity.

Quit comparing yourself to me and get a clue!

I got knocked down, and in time you will too!

I got up before 3 when you left at 2.

You put your money on the wrong contender, dude.

Wished I stayed gone so you can be the boss. I was on pause, but I come back hard!

You've got a locked jaw because you went by what you heard.

I'm back writing rhymes, going for the jugular.

No more kissing ass, now it's your turn.

Not right now! There's a line. You must wait your turn!

BY Z.E. FREY

The better you do, the more they wish they were you.

The best revenge is happiness.

What they've been always trying to prevent.

Thinking what I have coming to me, belongs to them?

What I need is David's rock to massacre them!

I suppose my vulnerability allowed them to get me, now I'm up to bat.

My turn now.

You've had your chance.

What's meant for me is meant to be.

Quit fighting my destiny.

You're acting wicked.

Don't get it twisted.

According to me and the powers that be

I haven't lost

One

Damn

Thing!

Sticks and Stones
Conquering Haters with Poetry

KARMA

Shut up! Be quiet! Don't say anything! Keep your mouth shut, you don't know what's going on, you only know half of the story and no one was talking to you anyway!

It's none of your business! Don't you have something productive to do?

Why don't you check your own home?

Oh. My. God!

WOW.

OK.

Whatever.

Really?

Hmph.

Unbelievable! The nerve. The audacity. It's just so sad, just too bad, that dudes been had, that girl, her bad. But I've had,

It up to here. So, don't bring that gossip in my ear.

If you've got a problem with me, don't even bother me. Don't pretend you are glad to see me because you never really liked me because I'm destined to be the victor like Nike.

BY Z.E. FREY

Appeasing no man. I'm not a fan of that band. I march to my own tune because no man was in the tomb. I don't monkey see, monkey do, because when I tried that, no one came to my rescue.

When animals attack, I maul and bite back. No mercy for my enemy because they never were a friend to me. The only way I'll be nice is by sparing your life, your reputation, that is. Be glad for that. I could've done worse than that, but the consequences weren't worth all that, so I'll let karma get at that ass and

laugh,

laugh,

laugh!

STICKS AND STONES
CONQUERING HATERS WITH POETRY

NOT MUCH TIME

I've been out and about, overseas so

please don't bring that mess about what you think is best for me.

If you want to kick it, then just say it instead of pretending like you want it.

A relationship, that is so don't get it twisted.

I'm about my business and my business has a purpose.

I fight to avoid lust because

Lust can have you acting in a crazy way.

I've got things to do and things to say.

So, go ahead, try to make my day.

Time is ticking.

What are you trying to say?

I really don't have all day.

Short, sweet, and to the point:

What's taking so long with this? Do you think this is a sport?

I will not fall subject to your confusion.

by Z.E. Frey

Your rambling is no longer amusing. I've got things to do and

You're slowing me up.

Hurry up!

Get to the point!

I don't belong to you!

Yes, I am your friend but

Don't you have something to do?

While you are telling me what's happening,

blessings are passing.

I cringe in just asking you a question.

Your answer is a guessing game of explanations seasoned with a hint of complaining and

that's making me a little nerved out.

I'm looking at my watch.

What ARE you talking about?

STICKS AND STONES
CONQUERING HATERS WITH POETRY

THE MESSENGER

I don't have a lot, but I don't have a little bit.

Haters talk more crap than a little bit!

Yes, I've got money. Yep, I've got cars. I even have a dude, I fit nicely on his arm!

But it's not about him, it's about me. You're staring so hard, take a picture, say cheese!

I call the shots because faith has my back. Under the radar, but I'll get right back.

Chill out kid, you're having a panic attack. I overcome. They don't know how to act.

To those who don't like me, you can bite me. Don't even approach me, you disgust me!

No need to pretend you're better than me. Don't waste my time, don't even talk to me!

But you'll probably be in my face like "It really wasn't me," fake me with a hug, now I have to shower see!

In the past, you never befriended me. I even caught you rolling your eyes at me!

Your pretending to like me is a pitiful sight to see.

I can't imagine how your anger came to be, but you better fix it with God you can really see,

BY Z.E. FREY

I'm not your friend, nor your enemy. You better check your p's and q's honestly.

I speak and recite verses for MY KING.

ITCHES

I think this itch might have a problem with me because, suddenly, I'm sensing some animosity and her little clique seems to have a distaste toward me and I can't think why that may be.

One thing I do know is these itches have a problem with me.

Because they're downright mean and they don't even know me much less sit down to have a conversation with me.

Yet, they've concluded I'm this and that and have excluded us from ever being able to understand one another because somehow they've figured that because I'm different,

I have the itch?

I've had to scratch and claw my way out of the generational curse of poverty, the "I'm not good enough" mentality, all by myself with nobody's help. Fought to

BY Z.E. FREY

maintain celibacy, minding my own business while working on my degree and still...

These itches have a problem with ME?!?

Well, excuse me!

I'm use to people having closed-door conversations about me. Instead of speculating, why not ask me? You'll find because I don't freely give up information does not mean I will not answer a question.

Ask me no questions and I won't tell you why, but I just can't figure out why these itches have a problem with me!

You know what?

I don't even know their names.

STICKS AND STONES
CONQUERING HATERS WITH POETRY

THE REMEDY

Irrelevant stress. I find it best to shake it off. Flush it down the sewer. Here's a prescription: Go on to something newer. Folks don't have a clue. I'm the more, you are the few. I'm the ace, you're the deuce. Schooling you with prophetic words. Watch me rise to the top like something frothy. Stronger than coffee.

Take two chill pills, and don't call me!

Can't stop me. Omega, but I'm not finished. I'm just getting started.

Late bloomers, early consumers, they farted. Shooting early out the chamber. Blocking, trigger-jamming, debris back-fired in your hand. You know, but cram to understand. Got a pen, but you don't want the mic in my hand. I school the insane membrane with intellectual soul-sifting, mood shiftin', make you think about it for a minute while I'm still chillin'.

You're stressing about something I was on last minute!

But can you dig it and forget it, because I did it. Now, let's squash this short. It's insignificant.

No qualms, bygones, be gone with all this stressing. It's a mess and we've got one life to live, so be happy. Brush it off like dandruff cause life's already rough. Don't sweat the small stuff. Be gone with that drama. I write it off, so why live it? Sift it. Shine or be a victim of this oral trigger.

BY Z.E. FREY

I deliver rhymes like a surgical incision.

Like a scalpel slits the skin,

I bleed through the pen.

Eject!

Inject!

Like a needle in the vein.

Sew you up for recovery and possibly rehabilitation

from all that unnecessary hating which brought you irrelevant stress in the first place!

Sticks and Stones
CONQUERING HATERS
...with poetry

BY Z.E. FREY

**Other books
By
Z. E. Frey**

I Won't Apologize for Being a Woman

*I Won't Apologize for Being a Woman
(Special Edition)*

Conquering Haters

Sticks and Stones, Conquering Haters…with poetry

*Open. Candid Haikus about Everyday Life
Coming Soon!*

iwa.yolasite.com

STICKS AND STONES
CONQUERING HATERS WITH POETRY

Purchase

I.W.A.

I WON'T APOLOGIZE!

Clothing and Accessories

at

cafepress.com/IWONTAPOLOGIZE

BY Z.E. FREY

What does I.W.A. mean?

I.W.A. stands for "I Won't Apologize".

An individual must take ownership in standing up for themselves and voicing their opinion. Overall, a person ought not apologize for finding their identity, building and sustaining self-confidence, promoting a positive self-esteem, and giving credit where it is due, all the while remaining diligent in self-improvement.

Voice your opinions and beliefs through I.W.A.

www. iwa. yolasite. com

Made in the USA
Charleston, SC
03 January 2013